the Australian
worship collection

the Australian worship collection

Kevin Mayhew

We hope you enjoy the music in this book. Further copies are available
from your local music shop or Christian bookshop.

In case of difficulty, please contact the publisher direct by writing to:

The Sales Department
KEVIN MAYHEW LTD
Buxhall
Stowmarket
Suffolk
IP14 3BW

Phone 01449 737978
Fax 01449 737834
E-mail info@kevinmayhew.com

Please ask for our complete catalogue of outstanding Church Music.

First published in Great Britain in 1998 by Kevin Mayhew Ltd.

This compilation © Copyright 1998 Kevin Mayhew Ltd.

ISBN 1 84003 205 7
ISMN M 57004 401 6
Catalogue No: 1450104

1 2 3 4 5 6 7 8 9

Cover design by Jaquetta Sergeant

Compiled by Jonathan Bugden and Matthew Lockwood

Music Editor: Donald Thomson
Music setting by Rob Danter and Vernon Turner

Printed and bound by Colorcraft Hong Kong

Foreword

Worship is our immediate response to a revelation of the grace and mercy of God expressed to us in Christ. As we gaze at the wonder of the cross, the unconditional love and compassion, we cannot help ourselves, we worship. This worship is expressed in many ways. Our lives change, hearts are softened, having been forgiven we become forgiving, having received grace and mercy we become gracious and merciful. Our hearts and lives are full of new songs.

Over the past twelve years these new songs have made their way from the songwriter's heart into the hearts and lives of congregations throughout Australia and now the world. These songwriters, inspired by the forgiveness and freedom that they have found in Jesus, have become the psalmist to a new generation of worshippers. Their songs have become the anthems of liberated hearts and lives.

This songbook is a collection of these anthems. They are Australian songs, written from Australian hearts, touched and changed by the heart of God, to the praise of his glorious grace.

GEOFF BULLOCK

Worship is not about great songs or great music. It is about you, your heart and your relationship with God. It is an act of pure adoration, where above all else, whatever is happening in our lives – we will worship God, the King of kings, my closest friend and the Saviour of our lives.

Worship: so much is written and said on the subject, yet many times you can miss the very reason why we do what we do. It's all because of Jesus – his love, his grace, his provision, the price he paid. Let this book encourage you to look to Christ . . . more of him and less of you.

DARLENE ZSCHECH

Important Copyright Information

The Publishers wish to express their gratitude to the copyright owners who have granted permission to include their copyright material in this book. Full details are clearly indicated on the respective pages.

The **words** of most of the songs in this publication are covered by a **Church Copyright Licence** which allows local church reproduction on overhead projector acetates, in service bulletins, songsheets, audio/visual recording and other formats.

The **music** in this book is covered by the newly introduced 'add-on' **Music Reproduction Licence** issued by CCL (Europe) Ltd and you may photocopy the music and words of the songs in this book provided:

You hold a current Music Reproduction Licence from CCL (Europe) Ltd.

The copyright owner of the hymn or song you intend to photocopy is included in the Authorised Catalogue List which comes with your Music Reproduction Licence.

Full details of both the Church Copyright Licence and the additional Music Reproduction Licence are available from:

Christian Copyright Licensing (Europe) Ltd, PO Box 1339, Eastbourne, East Sussex, BN21 4YF. Tel: 01323 417711, fax: 01323 417722, e-mail: info@ccli.com, web: www.ccli.com.

Please note, all texts and music in this book are protected by copyright and if you do <u>not</u> possess a licence from CCL (Europe) Ltd, they may <u>not</u> be reproduced in any way for sale or private use without the consent of the copyright owner.

Every effort has been made to trace the owners of copyright material, and we hope that no copyright has been infringed. Pardon is sought and apology made if the contrary be the case, and a correction will be made in any reprint of this book.

1 Almighty God, my Redeemer
(All things are possible)

Al-migh-ty God, my Re-deem-er, my hid-ing-place,
My feet are plant-ed on this rock and I will not

my safe re-fuge, no o-ther name like Je-sus,
be sha-ken. My hope, it comes from you a-lone,

1.
no pow'r can stand a-gainst you.

2.
my Lord, and my

sal-va-tion.

Your praise is al-ways on my lips,
You fill my life with grea-ter joy,

your word is liv - ing in my heart   and I   will praise
yes, I   de - light my - self   in   you

you with a new song,   my soul will bless   you, Lord.

you, Lord.   you, Lord. When I am

weak, you make   me   strong.

When I'm poor, I know I'm rich, for in the

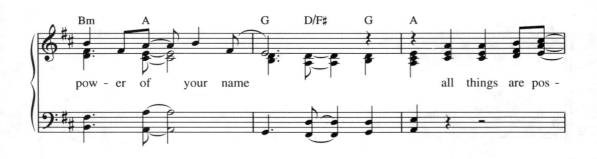

pow - er of your name all things are pos -

- si - ble, all things are pos - si - ble,

all things are pos - si - ble, all things are pos - si - ble.

Words and Music: Darlene Zschech

2 As for me, God came and found me
(God is in the house)

As for me and my house, we're gon-na serve the Lord.

As for I've got

Je - sus, Je - sus, he calls me for his own,

and he lifts me, lifts me a -

bove the world I know. God is in the house, there is

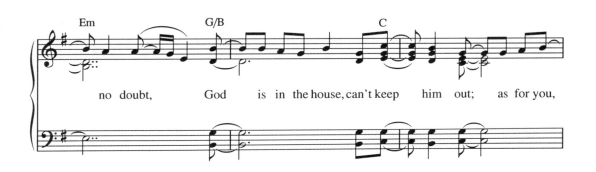

no doubt, God is in the house, can't keep him out; as for you,

as for me, we're gon-na serve the Lord.

As for

Words and Music: Russell Fragar and Darlene Zschech

3 Because of your love

Words and Music: Russell Fragar

4 Before the world began
(So you would come)

come. Come to the Fa – ther though your gift is small,

bro-ken hearts, bro-ken lives, he will take them all. The

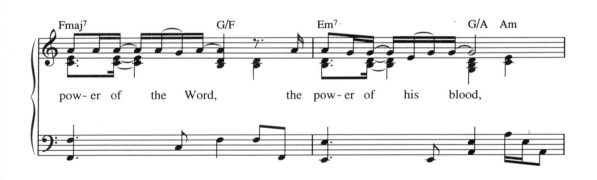

pow- er of the Word, the pow- er of his blood,

ev – 'ry-thing was done so you would come.

Words and Music: Russell Fragar

Praise be to the God and Father
of our Lord Jesus Christ!
In his great mercy
he has given us new birth into a living hope
through the resurrection of Jesus Christ from the dead.

1 Peter 1:3

5 Blessed be the Lord

he set me free.

Hea-ven shall hear the right-eous cry,

the earth shall shake at his com-mand.

Bless-ed be my Lord,

bless - ed be my rock,

bless - ed be my Sa - viour, heal - er, re -

deem - er Lord.

Bless -

Words and Music: Geoff Bullock

6 Blessing, honour, glory to the Lamb
(Glory to the Lamb)

Bless- ing, hon - our, glo - ry to the

Lamb. Ho - ly, right - eous,

wor - thy is the Lamb. Lamb.

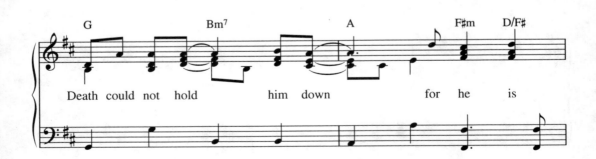

Death could not hold him down for he is

ri - sen.   Seat-ed up-on   the throne

he is   the   Lamb   of God.

Words and Music: Geoff Bullock and Dave Reidy

7 Can't stop talking

Can't stop talk-ing 'bout ev-'ry-thing he's done, it's the

best thing hap-pened since the world be - gun; it

did-n't come cheap but I got it for free, it's the hope of glo-ry

1. *and last time*   *Fine*   **2.**

Christ in me.   Christ in me. He helped me to see when my

Words and Music: Russell Fragar

But when the kindness and love
of God our Saviour appeared,
he saved us,
not because of righteous things we had done,
but because of his mercy.
He saved us through the washing of rebirth and renewal
by the Holy Spirit,
whom he poured out on us generously
through Jesus Christ our Saviour,
so that, having been justified by his grace,
we might become heirs
having the hope of eternal life.

Titus 3:4-7

8 Come on everyone, on your feet
(He shall be called)

1. Come on ev - 'ry-one, on your feet (come on ev - 'ry one, on your feet).
Je - sus rules in-side your heart (when Je - sus rules in-side your heart).

This is good news, sounds so sweet (this is good news, sounds so sweet).
That is where his king - dom starts (that is where his king-dom starts).

Je - sus is the Lord of all (Je - sus is the Lord of all) and
Je - sus is the com - ing King (Je - sus is the com - ing King) and

1.
he will ans - wer when you call (and he will ans - wer when you call). 2.When
this is what the an - gels sing (and

Words and Music: Russell Fragar

9 Day by day
(I am carried)

2. Mercy's healing grace relieving
   every spot and every stain.
   Forgiven freely, no more guilty,
   love has conquered shame.
   The broken mended, night has ended,
   lost and lonely, lost no more;
   for I am carried in the arms of
   grace and love divine.

3. Never worthy, never earning,
   all my works now left behind.
   Ever onwards, ever upwards,
   you've called me on to rise
   above my darkness, all my failure,
   every fear and every pain.
   Always carried, always covered by
   grace and love divine.

Words and Music: Geoff Bullock

Therefore God exalted him to the highest place
and gave him the name that is above every name,
that at the name of Jesus every knee should bow,
in heaven and on earth and under the earth,
and every tongue confess that Jesus Christ is Lord,
to the glory of God the Father.

Philippians 2:9-11

10 Every nation, power and tongue
(People just like us)

Words and Music: Russell Fragar

11 Every new day your glory unfolds
(My greatest love is you)

Words and Music: Russell Fragar

12 Father of life, draw me closer
(Let the peace of God reign)

Words and Music: Darlene Zschech

To him who is able to keep you from falling
and to present you before his glorious presence
without fault and with great joy –
to the only God our Saviour
be glory, majesty, power and authority,
through Jesus Christ our Lord, before all ages,
now and for evermore! Amen.

Jude 24-25

13 Forgetting what lies behind
(We're going on)

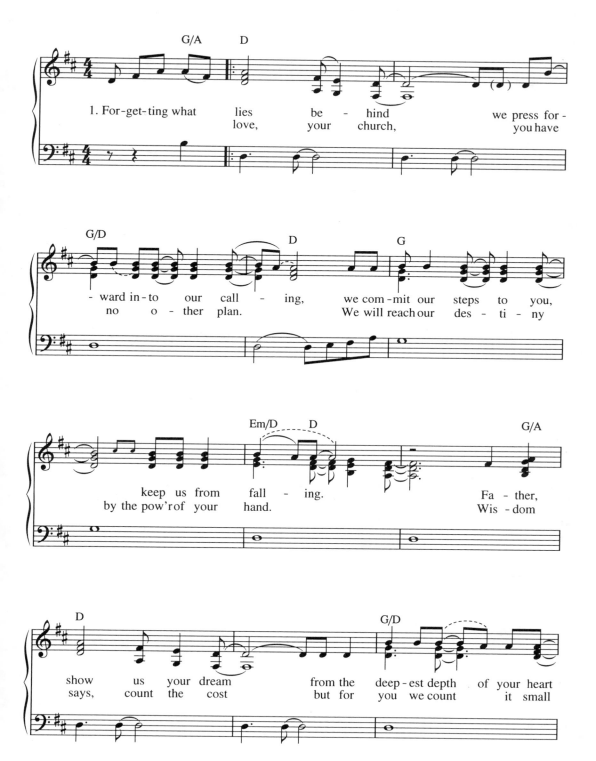

1. For-get-ting what lies be-hind, we press for-ward in-to our call - ing, we com-mit our steps to you, keep us from fall - ing. Fa - ther, show us your dream from the deep - est depth of your heart

love, your church, you have no o - ther plan. We will reach our des - ti - ny by the pow'r of your hand. Wis - dom says, count the cost but for you we count it small

moun - tains.   in   the   name of your Son

we're go - ing on.   2. This   is   your

we're go-ing on,   we're go-ing

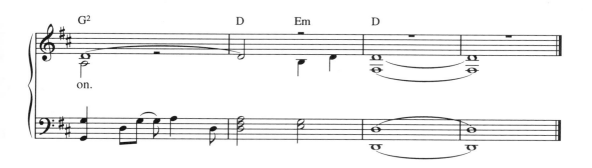

on.

Words and Music: Russell Fragar

14 Glory to the King of kings

2. Jesus, Lord, with eyes unveiled
   we will see your throne.
   Jesus, Prince of Peace,
   Son of God, Emmanuel.

Words and Music: Geoff Bullock

15 God is moving by his Spirit
(Revival)

1. God ... is mov-ing by his Spi-rit,
2. God ... is look-ing for a peo-ple

mov-ing 'cross the na - tion,
will-ing to be read - ied,

mov-ing 'cross our
read - y to o -

1. land.

2. bey.

And there will rise like a rush-ing wind, we'll

hear the Spi - rit's cry - y - y: Re-vi-val in our

Words and Music: Geoff Bullock

16 Hear these praises from a grateful heart
(Love you so much)

1. Hear these prais-es from a grate-ful heart, each time I think of you the prais-es start; love you so much, Je-sus, love you so much. so much. How my soul longs for

2. Lord, I love you,
   my soul sings
   in your presence, carried on your wings;
   love you so much, Jesus,
   love you so much.

Words and Music: Russell Fragar

17 He can make a way where there isn't a way
(The love of God can do)

Words and Music: Christine and Russell Fragar

I will extol the Lord at all times;
his praise will always be on my lips.
My soul will boast in the Lord;
let the afflicted hear and rejoice.
Glorify the Lord with me:
let us exalt his name together.
I sought the Lord, and he answered me;
he delivered me from all my fears.
Those who look to him are radiant;
their faces are never covered with shame.
This poor man called, and the Lord heard him;
he saved him out of all his troubles.
The angel of the Lord encamps
around those who fear him,
and he delivers them.
Taste and see that the Lord is good;
blessed is the man who takes refuge in him.

Psalm 34:1-8

18 He is able to wound
(Fall upon your knees)

1. He is a-ble to wound, he is able to heal, he is a-ble to re-prove, he is a-ble to for-give.

2. Though your spi-rit may be wound-ed, or your heart be filled with grief, wea-ry, he gives pow'r to the weak,

Words and Music: Miriam Webster

19 Here I am
(Hear me calling)

1. Here I am, reach-ing out I need you now O
2. And oh, my God

Lord, I come to you.

And I will reach

out, lift my hands to you. Hear me call-

ing your name. Take me

Words and Music: Geoff Bullock

20 He's the author of salvation
(Author of salvation)

He's the auth-or of sal-va-tion, Son of right-eous-ness,

Al-pha and O-me-ga, the be-gin-ning and the end.

He's the liv-ing re-ve-la-tion of the pow-er and the

glo-ry of the Lord.

We cry glo-ry and hon-our,

Words and Music: Geoff Bullock

Worthy is the Lamb, who was slain,
to receive power and wealth and
wisdom and strength
and honour and glory and praise!

Revelation 5:12

21 Holy One of God

Words and Music: Geoff Bullock

22 Holy Spirit, come

Ho - ly Spi - rit, come,

Ho - ly Spi - rit, come.

Heal our hearts, our lives,

cleanse our thoughts, our minds.

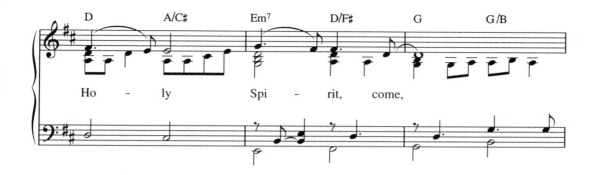

Ho — ly Spi - rit, come,

O come to us.

2. Holy Spirit, fall,
   Holy Spirit, fall.
   Drench us with your love,
   fill our lives with peace.
   Holy Spirit, fall,
   O fall on us.

3. Holy Spirit, flow,
   Holy Spirit, flow.
   Lead us in your will,
   empowered to proclaim.
   Holy Spirit, flow,
   O flow through us.

Words and Music: Geoff Bullock

23 Holy Spirit, rise

Words and Music: Geoff Bullock

24 I am not ashamed
(I'm saved)

I am not a-shamed of the gos-pel of his name, for it is the pow-er, the pow'r of my sal-va-tion, and I am not a-shamed of the gos-pel of his king-dom,

Words and Music: Geoff Bullock

25 I am pressing forward
(Born again)

2. I am looking up,
   no time for looking down,
   got my eyes on the Lord.

   We ain't hanging 'round,
   pressin' on to higher ground,
   movin' on and straight ahead.

   I feel his Spirit deep within,
   I got the power,
   he's forgiven my sin.

Words and Music: Geoff Bullock

No, in all these things
we are more than conquerors
through him who loved us.
For I am convinced that neither death nor life,
neither angels nor demons,
neither the present nor the future,
nor any powers,
neither height nor depth,
nor anything else in all creation,
will be able to separate us
from the love of God
that is in Christ Jesus our Lord.

Romans 8:37-39

26 I am walking on the way ahead
(Pressing on)

I am walk-ing on the way a-head, I am liv-

-ing all the truth you said. I am seek-

-ing for the high-er ground, 'cause I'm

liv-ing like I'm hea-ven bound. I am pray-

Words and Music: Geoff Bullock

27 I believe the promise

Words and Music: Russell Fragar

28 I bow my knee
(I'll love you more)

Words and Music: Rob and Debbie Eastwood

29 I draw near to you

Words and Music: Darlene Zschech and Reuben Morgan

30 I have heard of your fame
(Joy of the Lord)

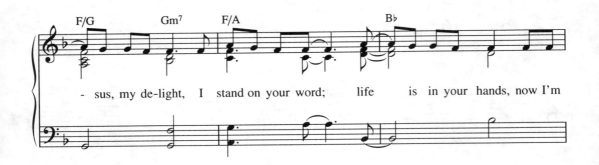

-sus, my de-light, I stand on your word; life is in your hands, now I'm

set-ting my eyes on you. Joy of the Lord will be my strength,

lift-ing me high a-bove my fears; know-ing the glo-

-ry of your ways, I'm re - joic - ing in your name.

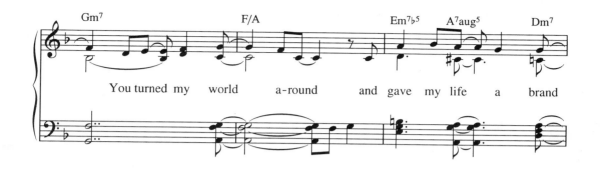

You turned my world a-round and gave my life a brand

new start. You took my bro – ken-ness and

turned it in – to some – thing good a-gain. I know

it, joy of the Lord will be my strength.

Words and Music: Reuben Morgan

31 I hear the sound of a holy war
(Your name)

Words and Music: Darlene Zschech

32 I just want to praise the Lord

Words and Music: Geoff Bullock

33 I know it

I know it, I know it, his blood has set me free, I've been de-li-vered, for-gi-ven, fear has got no hold on me. I'm set a-part, not liv-ing life my own way, no hold-ing back till I see him face to face be-cause I know it, oh yes, I

Words and Music: Darlene Zschech

And I pray that you,
being rooted and established in love,
may have power, together with all the saints,
to grasp how wide and long and high and deep
is the love of Christ,
and to know this love that surpasses knowledge –
that you may be filled to the measure
of all the fullness of God.

Ephesians 3:17-19

34 I'll take this time

I'll take this time,
Lord, to say I love you,
I'll take this time
to bow be-fore your throne.
throne. I'll take this time,

Words and Music: Geoff Bullock

35 I'll worship you

2. So, let these words
   reflect my heart,
   to make these songs
   be seen in me,
   and living life
   as living truth,
   in all I am,
   and hope to be.

Words and Music: Geoff Bullock

36 I'm changed, I'm not the same
(Father of lights)

Words and Music: Russell Fragar

37 I'm reaching out
(I believe)

I'm reach-ing out 'cause I know there's a bet-ter way; I walk by faith, I be-

lieve in a bet-ter day; I'm hold-ing on, hold-ing on to you.

I'm sing-ing out 'cause I've heard all the an-gels say; I can't hold back 'cause I

Words and Music: Geoff Bullock

38 I'm so secure
(In your hands)

Words and Music: Reuben Morgan

39 I'm your child

Words and Music: Geoff Bullock

40 I need you

I need you like a plan - et needs a sun.

I need you,

Jah - weh, Ho - ly One, I need you –

make the dark - ness run.

Be my God, I want you to, I need you.

You're a ri-ver in the des-ert sand, you're a

ship in a rag-ing flood. We're guid-ed by your migh-ty hand,

we live by your flesh and blood. You

teach your peo-ple how to sing, you teach your peo-ple how to fight,

you lead your peo - ple out; you're a cloud

D.S. al Fine

by day and a fire by night. I need you.

Words and Music: Russell Fragar

41 In my life proclaim your glory
(Lord of all mercy)

1. In my life pro-claim your glo - ry,
2. In my soul un - veil your love, Lord,

in my heart re-veal your ma - jes - ty,
deep with - in my heart re - new - ing me,

then my soul shall speak the won - ders of your grace, and this
day by day your life trans-form- ing all I am, as this

heart of mine shall sing your praise.
heart of mine re - flects your praise.

Words and Music: Geoff Bullock

42 In the name of the Lord

we have been re - leased in the name of the Lord.

1. Heal-ing to the na - tions, sal-

va-tion to the ends of the earth, pro-claim de-liv-'rance for his

king-dom comes in the name of the Lord.

2. Righteousness and honour,
the glory of the sons of God,
overcoming and victorious
in the name of the Lord.

Words and Music: Geoff Bullock

O God, you are my God,
earnestly I seek you;
my soul thirsts for you,
my body longs for you,
in a dry and weary land
where there is no water.

I have seen you in the sanctuary
and beheld your power and your glory.
Because your love is better than life,
my lips will glorify you.
I will praise you as long as I live,
and in your name I will lift up my hands.

Psalm 63:1-4

43 In the silence

1. In the si - lence of your maj - es - ty,
2. With the pow - er of your pre - sence

in the splen - dour of your ho - li - ness,
and your beau - ty all a - round,

in the still - ness of your glo - ry,
as the hea - vens stand in awe of you

let me hear your voice,

The gen-tle whis-per of your voice.

Let me hear your voice,

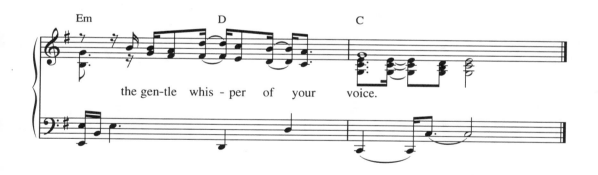

the gen-tle whis-per of your voice.

Words and Music: Paul Iannuzzelli

44 Into the shelter house I go
(Shelter house)

2. I am filled with the power and authority
   to take on any opposition that may rise.
   I don't care about the circumstance
   I may be in,
   'cause I know this power within me
   never ends.

Words and Music: Stephen McPherson

45 I trust in you, my faithful Lord
(I will bless you, Lord)

Words and Music: Darlene Zschech

46 I've been forgiven
(The stone's been rolled away)

Words and Music: Geoff Bullock

47 I've come to worship as I should
(I can't wait)

I can't wait to wor-ship the Lord. We praise your name,

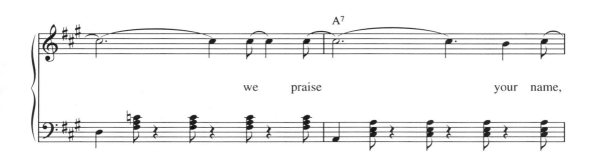

we praise your name,

we praise your name,

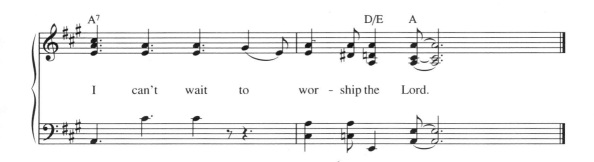

I can't wait to wor - ship the Lord.

Words and Music: Russell Fragar

To him who loves us
and has freed us from our sins by his blood,
and has made us to be a kingdom and priests
to serve his God and Father –
to him be glory and power for ever and ever!
Amen.

Revelation 1:5b-6

48 I've found a friend
(Joy in the Holy Ghost)

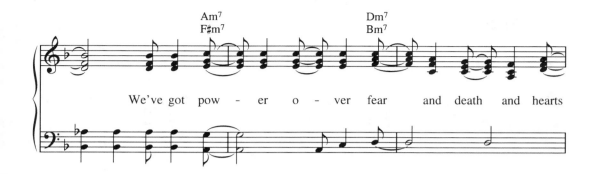

We've got pow - er o - ver fear and death and hearts

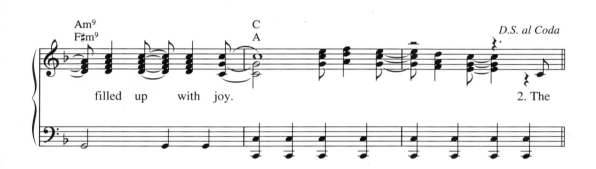

filled up with joy. 2. The

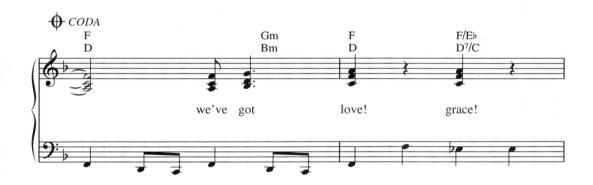

we've got love! grace!

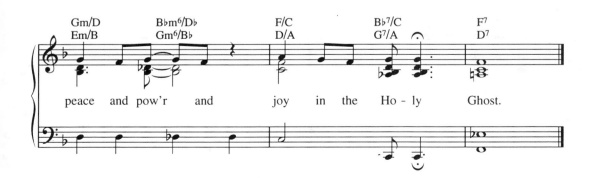

peace and pow'r and joy in the Ho - ly Ghost.

Words and Music: Russell Fragar

49 I want to be your hands
(Make me your servant)

I want to be your hands and be your feet.

Lord, make me your ser - vant. I want to

tell your love to ev - 'ry-one I meet.

Fine

Lord, make me your ser - vant.

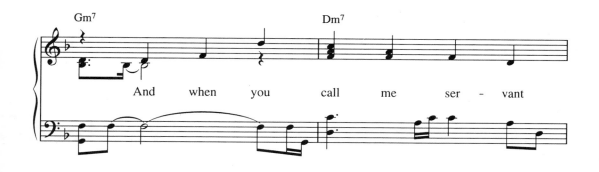

And when you call me ser - vant

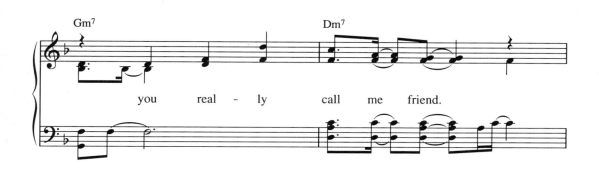

you real - ly call me friend.

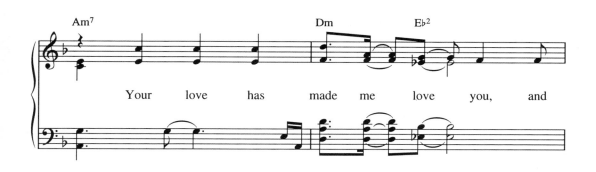

Your love has made me love you, and

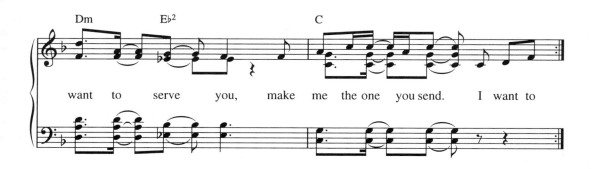

want to serve you, make me the one you send. I want to

Words and Music: Russell Fragar

Great and marvellous are your deeds,
Lord God Almighty.
Just and true are your ways,
King of the ages.
Who will not fear you, O Lord,
and bring glory to your name?
For you alone are holy.
All nations will come
and worship before you,
for your righteous acts have been revealed.

Revelation 15:3-4

50 I will behold the majesty of God

1. I will be - hold the ma-jes-ty of
   take of the right-eous-ness of
   hold the beau-ty of the

God, the ri - sen Prince of Peace;
God, re-demp-tion through your blood,
Lord, my eyes will sure - ly see

Son of right-eous-ness; you suf-fered for my
for-give-ness of my sin, the rich-es of your
my ears will sure-ly hear the trum-pet-call of

sin, with stripes you brought me heal -
grace, in wis - dom, un - der-stand -
God, the voice of the arch - an -

ing,   in death you brought me   life,   this life I now re -
ing,   the myst -'ry of your will   in Christ we see ful -
gel,   the glo - ry of the Lord,   the ri - sen Lamb of

ceive.
filled.   For you a-lone are wor - thy,
God.

and you have o -ver - come.   Death has been de -

feat   -   ed,   right-eous-ness has won;

cre - a - tion bows be - fore you, all hea - vens shout your

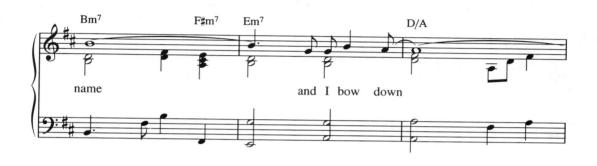

name and I bow down

and wor - ship you.

2. I will par -
3. I will be -

Words and Music: Geoff Bullock

51 I will come to you
(Lord, your goodness)

Words and Music: Reuben Morgan

52 I will lift my voice

2. I will lift my hands to the Lord of lords
   as an offering to him.
   I will lift my life to the Lord of lords
   as an offering to him.

Words and Music: Geoff Bullock

Be imitators of God, therefore,
as dearly loved children
and live a life of love,
just as Christ loved us
and gave himself up for us
as a fragrant offering and sacrifice to God.

Ephesians 5:1-2

53 I will never be the same again

Words and Music: Geoff Bullock

54 I will rest in Christ

hope in him, I will find a place of com-fort, I can

find a place of rest, held in love, loved in him,

safe, I am se-cure as I rest in Christ, as I

hope in him.

2. I am not dismayed
   I am not cast down
   I will never be alone
   I need never fear
   I can always hope
   I can always love
   for the love of God has
   touched my heart
   in him I am secure.

3. I will trust in Christ
   like a rock in stormy seas
   I have found a shelter in
   His life and peace in me.
   I have found the way,
   the truth; this perfect life,
   and the hope in me,
   is found in him
   the lover of my soul.

Words and Music: Geoff Bullock

55 I will worship you

Words and Music: Geoff Bullock

56 Jesus, fill me with your love
(With your love)

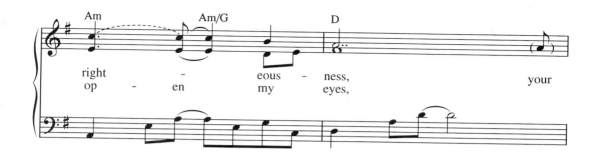

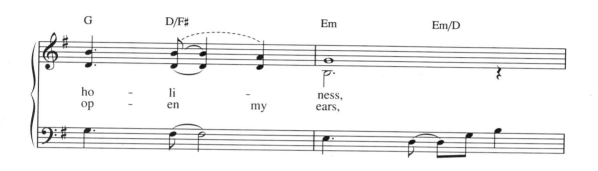

Words and Music: Geoff Bullock

57 Jesus, God's righteousness revealed
(This kingdom)

Je - sus, God's right-eous-ness re - vealed, the Son of Man, the Son of God, his king-dom comes. Je - sus, re - demp-tion's sac - ri - fice, now glo - ri - fied, now jus-ti - fied, his king-dom comes. And this

2. Jesus, the expression of God's love,
   the grace of God, the Word of God, revealed to us;
   Jesus, God's holiness displayed,
   now glorified, now justified, his kingdom comes.

Words and Music: Geoff Bullock

58 Jesus, Jesus

1. Je - sus, Je - sus,

one touch of your hand   I am healed and I   am whole.
one glimpse of your face   brings

fire   to   my soul.

Chorus

And, Je - sus,   I come

2. Jesus, Jesus,
   from darkness to light
   my life overflows.
   Jesus, Jesus,
   your mercy and grace
   like a river flowing down.

Words and Music: Geoff Bullock

59 Jesus, lover of my soul

I love you,   I need you,   though my world will fall,   I'll

ne - ver let   you go.   My   Sa - viour,

my clos - est friend,   I will wor-ship you   un -

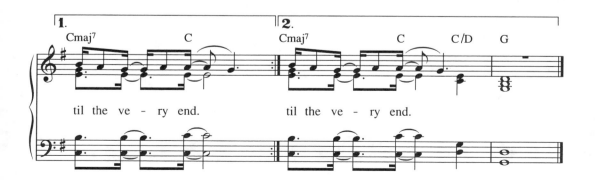

til the ve - ry end.   til the ve - ry end.

Words and Music: John Ezzy, Daniel Grul and Stephen McPherson

60 Jesus, what a beautiful name

Words and Music: Tanya Riches

61 Jesus, you're all I need

your-self   so I   could live,   you   are all   I need.

Oh, you pur – chased my   sal - va - tion   and

wiped a - way   my   tears,   now I drink your liv – ing wa-

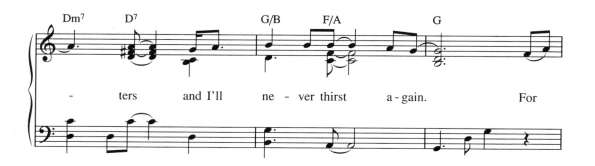

- ters   and I'll   ne - ver thirst a - gain.   For

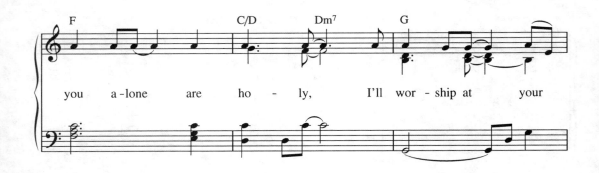

you a-lone are ho – ly, I'll wor-ship at your

throne and you will reign for e – ver,

ho – ly is the Lord. Je-sus, you're all

Words and Music: Darlene Zschech

Praise God in his sanctuary;
praise him in his mighty heavens.
Praise him for his acts of power;
praise him for his surpassing greatness.

Psalm 150:1-2

62 Jesus, your loving kindness
(Your love)

Je - sus, your lov-ing kind-ness, I'm so blessed by all that you've done, this life that you give.

Je - sus, your lov - ing kind-ness is life that's chang-ing my heart, draw-ing me near to you. Your love is bet -

Words and Music: Reuben Morgan

63 Jump to the jam

Words and Music: Paul Iannuzzelli

64 Just let me say

hea-vens can trem-ble and fall. Just let me
sand is ho-ly gro-und and I am
called a child of God. Just makes me

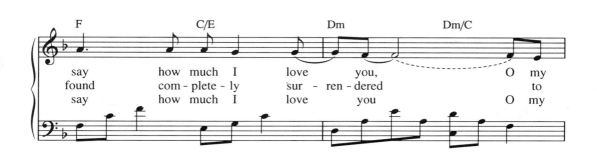

say how much I love you, O my
found com-plete-ly sur-ren-dered to
say how much I love you O my

to repeat

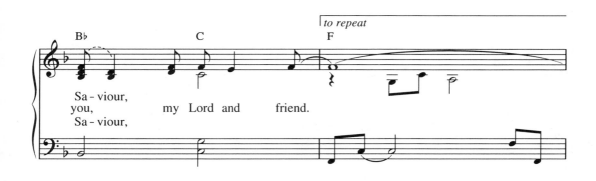

Sa-viour,
you, my Lord and friend.
Sa-viour,

last time

2. Just let me
3. So let me

Words and Music: Geoff Bullock

65 King of kings

King of kings, Lord of lords,

Je-sus, the Son of God is glo-ri-fied,

Prince of Peace, Ho-ly One,

Je-sus, the Son of God is glo-ri-fied.

last time

Fine

1. He is ri-sen to the

Fa - ther's right hand, now seat-ed on the throne, all au - tho - ri - ty in hea - ven and on earth is gi-ven in his name, the name of the Lord.

2. He's exalted 'bove the heavens and earth,
   and every knee shall bow,
   every tongue confess that
   Jesus Christ is Lord,
   the Name above all names,
   the name of the Lord.

Words and Music: Geoff Bullock

66 Lift high his name

Words and Music: Geoff Bullock

67 Longin' for your touch

Words and Music: Paul Iannuzzelli and Tim Uluirewa

O Lord, our Lord,
how majestic is your name in all the earth!
You have set your glory
above the heavens.

Psalm 8:1

68 Lord, I come to you
(Power of your love)

1. Lord, I come to you, let my heart be changed, re - newed, flow - ing from the grace that I found in you.

2. Lord, un - veil my eyes, let me see you face to face, the know - ledge of your love as you live in me.

And, Lord, I've come to know
Lord, re - new my mind

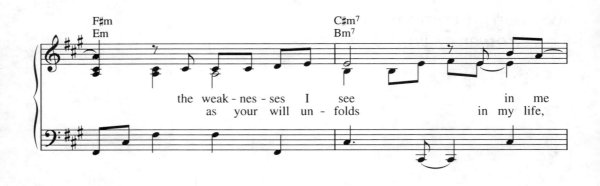

the weak - nes - ses   I   see   in   me
as   your will un - folds   in my life,

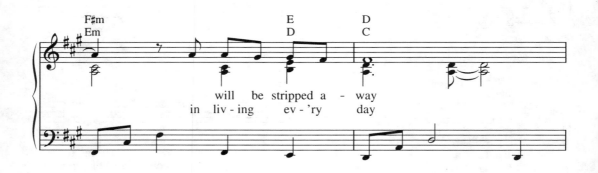

will   be stripped a - way
in liv - ing ev - 'ry day

by the pow'r of your love.
in the pow'r of your love.

Chorus

Hold   me close,   let your love sur - round

Words and Music: Geoff Bullock

69 Lord, I give my life to you
(Surrender)

2. Lord, I give my dreams, my plans,
everything and all I am,
I surrender.
And I bring my love for you,
there's nothing I can do,
I surrender.
As a living sacrifice,
you've come to give me life
and the love that overwhelms my soul.
So I bring this heart, this life,
the troubles and the strife,
I surrender.

Words and Music: Geoff Bullock

70 Lord, I give myself

You com - fort me and ev-'ry- where that I go I'm

not a - lone, migh - ty God. I know you're

with me, and ev-'ry - where that I go I'm

not a - lone, migh - ty God. I know you're with me.

Words and Music: Darlene Zschech

71 Lord, I lift my voice in praise to you
(Jesus, you gave it all)

1. Lord, I lift my voice in praise to you for the
ev-'ry breath that comes from me the will

love you placed in - side of me, Lord, I
flow your mer - cy and of your grace. Pro -

give my life, my heart and soul to you a -
claim-ing love and li - ber - ty, for

lone. 2. And with all who have an ear to hear. And your love

stirs faith and hope in me, and your

Words and Music: Craig Gower

72 Lord, I long to see you glorified
(Lord of all)

1. Lord, I long to see you glorified in ev'ry-thing I do. All my heart-felt dreams I put a-side to see your Spi-rit move with pow-er in my life.

2. Je-sus, Lord of all e-ter-ni-ty, your child-ren rise in faith. All the earth dis-plays your glo-ry and each word you speak brings life to all who hear. Lord of

all,   all of cre - a - tion sings your praise   in

hea-ven and earth.   Lord, we stand   hearts o - pen wide,   be ex -

al - ted.

Words and Music: Steve McPherson

73 Lord, I'm holding on to you
(Holding on)

Lord, I'm hold-ing on to you, Je-sus, clo-ser and clo-ser to you and in all that I am and in ev-'ry-thing I do I'm hold-ing on to you.

Words and Music: Geoff Bullock

74 Lord, I want to know you more
(Show your glory)

Lord, I want to know you more, let your
word re-new my mind, and, Lord, I want to love you
more, let your Spi - rit heal my heart.
Teach me, lead me, work your will through

me,   help   me,   guide   me.

Lord,   show   your   glo -   ry,   show   your

glo -   ry.

2. Lord, I want to worship you
with more than words alone,
and, Lord, I want to serve you more,
your life revealed in me.
Take me, make me a
vessel for your love,
shake me, break me.
Lord, show your glory,
show your glory.

Words and Music: Geoff Bullock

75 Lord, my heart cries out
(Glory to the King)

Lord, my heart cries out, glo-ry to the King, my great-est love in life. I hand you ev-'ry-thing. Glo-ry, glo-ry, I hear the an-gels sing. O-pen my ears, let me hear your voice to know that sweet sound. O, my soul, re-joice. Glo-ry,

Words and Music: Darlene Zschech

76 Lord of Creation

Words and Music: Geoff Bullock

77 Lord of the heavens

Words and Music: Lucy Fisher

78 Lord, we come to you

Words and Music: Geoff Bullock

Come, let us bow down in worship,
let us kneel before the Lord our Maker;
for he is our God
and we are the people of his pasture,
the flock under his care.

Psalm 95:6-7

79 Lord, we proclaim you now
(Let your presence fall)

Words and Music: David Willersdorf

80 My God can never fail
(He's real!)

1. My God can ne-ver fail, he's been proved
3. Got dreams, turn them in-to plans too big for

time and a-gain. Trust him, you'll see he's got all the pow'r you need.
hu-man hands.

after v.3 cut to Chorus

2. He's ne-ver ear-ly, ne-ver late,

He's real! Faith's a lot strong-er than what you feel.

He's real! He's real! I'm be-liev-in' for mi-ra - cles.

D.S. al Coda

CODA

all the pow'r you need, all the pow'r you need.

Words and Music: Russell Fragar

81 My heart sings praises

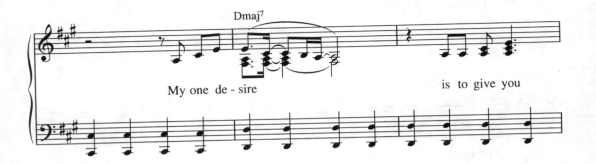

My one de - sire   is to give you

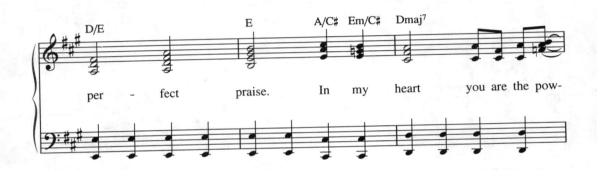

per - fect   praise.   In   my   heart   you are the pow-

- er,   in my night   ne-ver-fail - ing light.   With ev - 'ry

breath that I take I'll de -clare   the things   you've done.

Words and Music: Russell Fragar

82 My Jesus, my Saviour
(Shout to the Lord)

Words and Music: Darlene Zschech

83 My spirit rests in you
(Shadow of your wings)

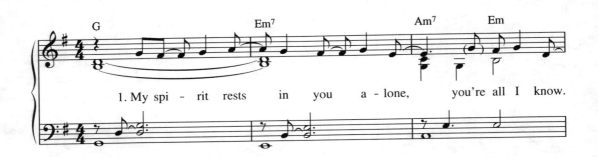

1. My spi - rit rests in you a - lone, you're all I know.

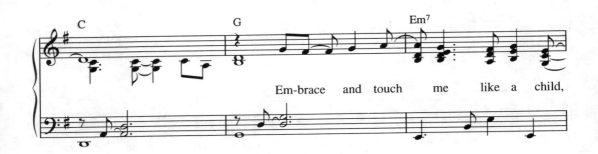

Em-brace and touch me like a child,

I'm safe in you. You're my shel - ter through it all,

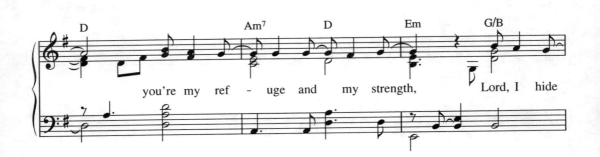

you're my ref - uge and my strength, Lord, I hide

in the sha - dow of your wings.

You're my shel - ter through it all, you're my ref -

- uge and my strength, Lord, I hide in the sha-

- dow of your wings.

2. My Lord, you're faithful,
   you supply all good things,
   you know completely
   all my thoughts,
   my deepest needs.

Words and Music: Reuben Morgan

84 O Holy Spirit

1. O Ho - ly Spi - rit, Spi - rit of God,
2. O Ho - ly Spi - rit, Spi - rit of grace,

pu - ri - fy - ing fire,
sanc - ti - fy - ing fire,

trans - form - ing power.
re - fin - ing flame.

O Ho - ly
O Ho - ly

Spi - rit,
Spi - rit,

o - ver - whelm my heart
sa - tu - rate my soul

and let your

Words and Music: Geoff Bullock

85 Oh, the mercy of God

2. Oh, the richness of grace, the depths of his love,
   in him is redemption, the forgiveness of sin.
   You called us as righteous, predestined in him
   for the praise of his glory, included in Christ.

3. Oh, the glory of God expressed in his Son,
   his image and likeness revealed to us all;
   the plea of the ages completed in Christ,
   that we be presented perfected in him.

Words and Music: Geoff Bullock

86 O Lord, you have searched my heart
(Within your love)

O Lord, you have searched my heart, you have known my thoughts, my ways.

You guide each step 'til it leads to you and I am

found safe with-in your love. Hold me now

safe with-in your arms, hold me clo-

2. O Lord, where can I hide
   from this love that can know no end?
   I am found in this state of grace,
   I am found within your love.

Words and Music: Geoff Bullock

87 O Lord, you lead me
(Have faith in God)

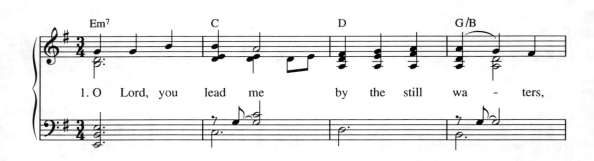

1. O Lord, you lead me by the still wa- ters,

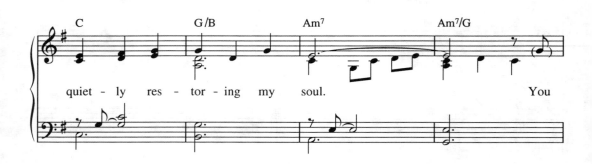

quiet- ly res- tor- ing my soul. You

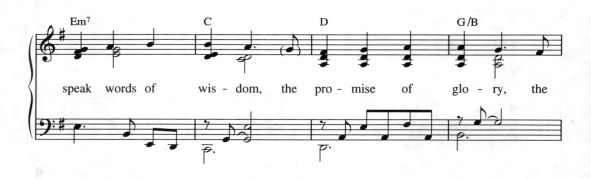

speak words of wis- dom, the pro- mise of glo- ry, the

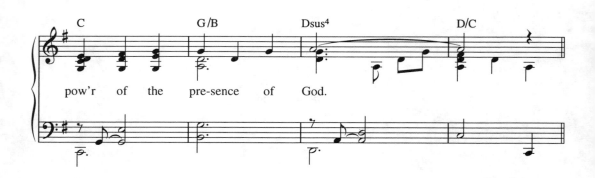

pow'r of the pre- sence of God.

2. O Lord, you guide me
through all the darkness,
turning my night into day;
you'll never leave me,
never forsake me
the pow'r of the presence of God.

Words and Music: Geoff Bullock

In him the whole building is joined together
and rises to become a holy temple in the Lord.
And in him you too are being built together
to become a dwelling in which God lives by his Spirit.

Ephesians 2:21-22

88 One hope

Words and Music: Darlene Zschech and Russell Fragar

89 Open arms
(I belong to you)

1. O - pen arms   wel-come me close   to your heart,
2. Take my life,   join me for e - ver with you;

and there I long   to   stay.   Mer-cy falls,
make our hearts   as   one.   Per-fect love,

cleans-ing my life   in your blood   whi - ter than the
driv-ing a - way   all my fears,   free - dom I've

snow.   I be-long to you,   Je-sus, my first love.
found.

Words and Music: Reuben Morgan

90 Our Father, who art in heaven

Words and Music: Rob Eastwood

91 Refresh my heart

by your Spi - rit, lift me up, Lord, re-fresh my heart.

And I will wor - ship you, Lord,

with all of my heart and I will fol -

- low you, Lord, re-fresh my heart,

re-fresh my heart.

Words and Music: Geoff Bullock

92 Rock of the ages

2. Al-pha O -   Lamb of God,

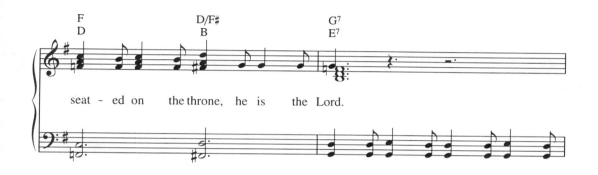

seat - ed on   the throne, he is   the Lord.

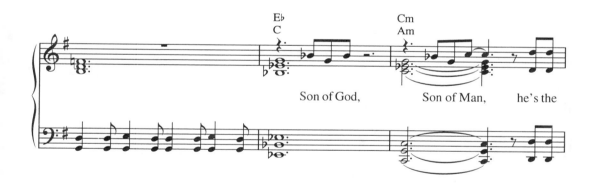

Son of God,   Son of Man,   he's the

Lord,   he's the King!   Hear   the an - gels sing.   Rock of the

Words and Music: Geoff Bullock and Darlene Zschech

As I looked,
thrones were set in place,
and the Ancient of Days took his seat.
His clothing was as white as snow;
the hair of his head was white like wool.
His throne was flaming with fire,
and its wheels were all ablaze.
A river of fire was flowing,
coming out from before him.
Thousands upon thousands attended him;
ten thousand times ten thousand stood before him.

Daniel 7:9-10a

93 Salvation

grace has res - cued me.
word trans - for-ming me. I've come to put my trust in the Lord.

2. Sal -

I'm walk-ing

step by step, I'm read -ing line by line.

Faith to faith I'm pray -ing all the time. I'm sing -ing,

Words and Music: Geoff Bullock

94 Show me your ways

Show me your ways that I may walk with you, show me your ways, I put my hope in you. The cry of my heart is to love you more, to live with the touch of your hand, stronger each day, show me your ways.

Words and Music: Russell Fragar

95 Standing in your presence
(I live to know you)

Words and Music: Darlene Zschech

96 The earth resounds in songs of praise
(We proclaim your kingdom)

Words and Music: Geoff Bullock

97 The enemy's defeated

The en-e-my's de - feat - ed, the bat-tle is the Lord's, the right-eous are for - gi - ven, the vic-to-ry is yours. Oh, the fire is spread-ing the glo-ry of the Lord,

Words and Music: Geoff Bullock and Lucy Fisher

98 The heavens shall declare

Words and Music: Geoff Bullock

99 The Holy Spirit is here
(Church on fire)

We have a burn - ing de-sire, to lift up Je - sus' name.

Let the fire burn in ev - 'ry heart, to light the way, de - feat

the dark. Let the flame of love burn high - er. This is a church,

this is a church on fire.

1.

D.S. **2.** *Fine*

1. The Ho-ly

2. Well there's a light that shines
   to make the darkness disappear,
   there's a power at work,
   but there's nothing to fear.
   Something very good,
   something good is going
   on around here.

Words and Music: Russell Fragar

100 The life of God has found a home in me
(No longer I)

1. The life of God has found a home in me,
2. call up-on the Name a-bove all names,
3. God has reached me from the cross,

I in my

live in Christ a-lone,
Je-sus Christ I stand;
sins now bu - ried there

this pre-cious
a con-
where no

mys-te-ry once hid-den now re-vealed,
fess-ion of the sav-ing grace of God,
me-mo-ry or con-dem-na-tion's pow'r

the
through the
can

hope of glo-ry now.
blood of Je-sus Christ.
leave a mark on me.

No long-er I

Words and Music: Geoff Bullock

Now the Lord is the Spirit,
and where the Spirit of the Lord is, there is freedom.
And we, who with unveiled faces all reflect the Lord's glory,
are being transformed into his likeness with ever-increasing glory,
which comes from the Lord, who is the Spirit.

2 Corinthians 3:17-18

101 The love of God, heaven's hope
(Unfailing love)

1. The love of God, hea-ven's hope,
this per - fect peace, this rest for my soul.
This love di-vine por-trayed in pain, the cross stands a - lone:
un-fail-ing love. love.
The love of God was found in the nails,

the love of God was seen in the scars.
The light and the life was dark- ened by death, my hope and sal -va - tion carr -ied to life: un -fail - ing love.

2. The love of God,
   creation's cry,
   perfection portrayed,
   broken for me.
   The author of life
   has suffered our pain,
   the cross stands alone:
   unfailing love.

3. The love of God,
   written in blood,
   this empty grave,
   the stone rolled away.
   The mercy of God
   has triumphed in Christ,
   the cross stands alone:
   unfailing love.

Words and Music: Geoff Bullock

102 There's a light that shines
(You call us near)

Celtic style

1. There's a light that shines, a lamp that burns, the hope, the peace of

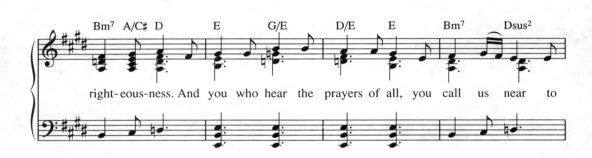

right-eous-ness. And you who hear the prayers of all, you call us near to

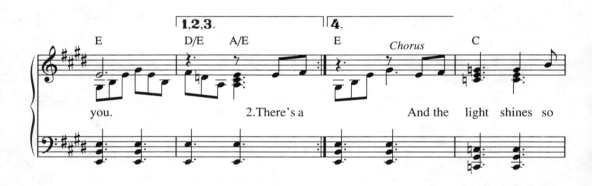

1,2,3. you. 2. There's a **4.** *Chorus* And the light shines so

we can see, and the truth came so

we   could   know.   And the   light   of

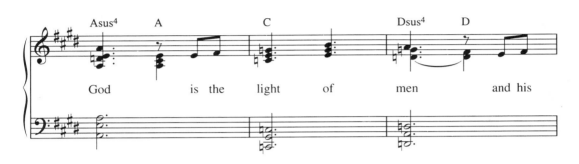

God   is the   light   of   men   and his

life   gives   life   to   all.

2. There's a path that leads,
   a way that's true,
   the light, the life,
   the perfect truth.
   We come to you forgiven, free,
   you call us near to you.

3. No other way,
   no other life,
   no other truth,
   no other light.
   The way ahead is found in Christ,
   you call us near to you.

4. We will dance and sing
   for freedom comes
   to heal our hearts
   and dry our tears.
   For evermore in glorious light,
   you call us near to you.

Words and Music: Geoff Bullock

103 There's a river
(Living waters)

There's a ri - ver, full of life, stream-ing from the heart of God.

There's a spi - rit, filled with love, flow-ing from the heart of God. Liv-ing

wa - ters, flood my soul. Liv-ing

Words and Music: Paul Iannuzzelli

104 The time has come for justice

1. The time has come for jus-tice, the time has come for peace,
time has come for mer-cy, the time has come for grace,
time has come for right-eous-ness, to shout it in the streets.
time has come for ev-'ry man for heal-ing and re-lease.

The

Chorus

The time has come, where
jus-tice will pre-vail, the time has come, his
truth will ne-ver fail. The king-doms of this world will fall,

2. The time has come for healing
   to reach across this land.
   Wounded spirits, broken hearts
   shall hear and understand
   that the time has come for mercy
   for justice and for peace,
   the time has come and freedom cries,
   in grace we find release.

Words and Music: Geoff Bullock

105 The word of God is planted
(People get free)

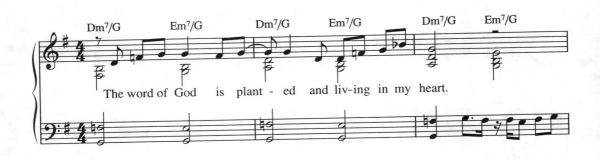

The word of God is plant-ed and liv-ing in my heart.

I'm an o - ver-com - er, I live his prom-ise

out. This was not a new

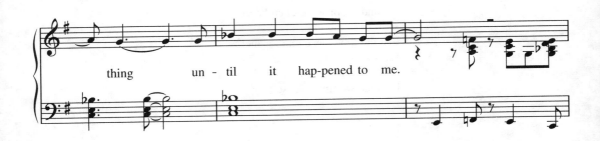

thing un - til it hap-pened to me.

You lose your tears when you trust his grace.

You lose your pain when you know his touch.

On-ly Christ can turn your bit - ter in-to sweet, peo-ple get

D.C. twice
2nd time to Coda

free!

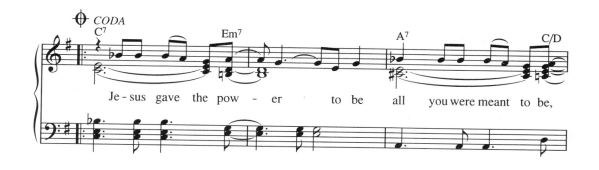

Je - sus gave the pow – er to be all you were meant to be,

and peo-ple get free! Peo-ple get free!

Peo - ple get free!

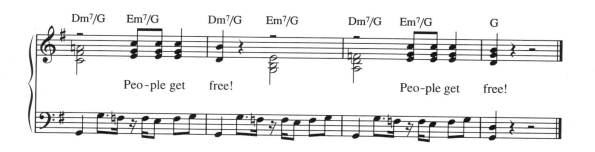

Peo-ple get free! Peo-ple get free!

Words and Music: Russell Fragar

106 This grace is mine
(The power and the glory)

1. This grace is mine, this glo - ry, earth-bound hea-ven sent this plan di-vine, this life, this light that breaks my night, the Spi-rit of God hea - ven falls like a dove to my heart.

1. *to verse 2*

2, 3. *Chorus*

The pow - er and the glo - ry of your name.

The pow-er and the glo - ry of your name.

The pow-er and the glo - ry of your name.

the name of the Lord, the Son of

D.C. verse 3 | *last time*

God.

2. This love is mine, so undeserved, this glorious name,
this Son, this God, this life, this death, this vict'ry won,
forgiveness has flowed and this grace that is mine finds my heart.

3. This life is mine, so perfect and so pure, this God in me,
this glorious hope from earth to heaven, death to life,
this future assured and secured by this love in my heart.

Words and Music: Geoff Bullock

107 This is my desire
(I give you my heart)

Words and Music: Reuben Morgan

108 This is our nation
(The great Southland)

1. This is our na-tion, this is our land, this is our fu-ture, this is our hope. A land of reap-ing, a land of har - vest, this is our land, this is our home. This is the

Chorus

great South - land of the Ho - ly Spi-rit, a land of

red dust plains and sum-mer rains, to this sun-burnt land we will see a flood, and to this

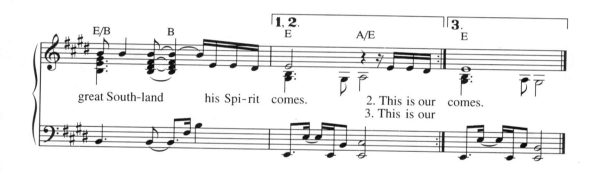

great South-land his Spi-rit comes. 2. This is our comes.
3. This is our

2. This is our nation, this is our land,
   this land of plenty, this land of hope.
   The richest harvest is in her peoples.
   We see revival, his Spirit comes.

3. This is our nation, this is our land,
   this lucky country of dreams gone dry,
   and to these peoples we see a harvest,
   and to this land revival comes.

Words and Music: Geoff Bullock

109 This is the hour
(Latter rain)

Words and Music: Geoff Bullock

110 This love, this hope
(Now is the time)

This love, this hope, this peace

of God, this right - eous - ness, this faith, this joy,

this life, com-plete in me. Now healed

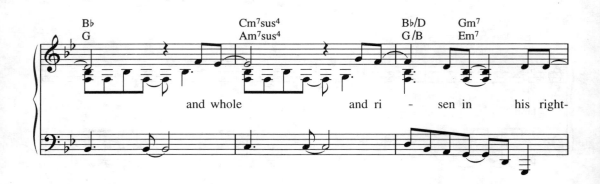

and whole and ri - sen in his right-

Words and Music: Geoff Bullock

111 Walking in the light

Words and Music: Darlene Zschech

My command is this:
Love each other as I have loved you.
Greater love has no one than this,
that he lay down his life for his friends.
You are my friends if you do what I command.
I no longer call you servants,
because a servant does not know his master's business.
Instead, I have called you friends,
for everything that I learned from my Father
I have made known to you.

John 15:12-15

112 We behold the Lamb of God

We be-hold the Lamb of God,

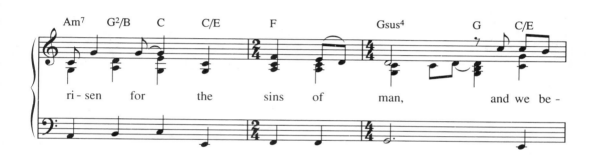

ri-sen for the sins of man, and we be-

hold him in ma-jes-ty, for

we be-hold the Lamb of God.

Words and Music: Geoff Bullock

113 We come into your presence
(Father of creation)

We come in-to your pre-sence to sing a song to you, a

song of praise and hon-our for all the things you've helped us through; you

gave a life worth liv-ing, a life in love with you, and

now I just love giv-ing all my prai-ses back to you. You're the

Words and Music: Robert Eastwood

114 Well, I was in need
(Friends in high places)

Words and Music: Russell Fragar

The Lord will surely comfort Zion
and will look with compassion on all her ruins;
he will make her deserts like Eden,
her wastelands like the garden of the Lord.
Joy and gladness will be found in her,
thanksgiving and the sound of singing.

Isaiah 51:3

115 We need reviving

Words and Music: Geoff Bullock

116 We're a generation saved by grace
(Steppin' out)

1. We're a ge-ne-ra - tion saved by grace and set a-part to change this land
2. We're the cho-sen few who speak his word, and ma-ni-fest it in our lives.

We're stand-ing strong and press-ing on, we know in Je - sus Christ we can.
We're not moved by what the world says, got Je - sus on our side.

The church of God is
We're not dis-mayed by what we

grow-ing ev - 'ry day we're tak-ing ground and
see with our eyes. we walk by faith

Words and Music: Stephen McPherson

117 We're gonna praise his holy name
(Praise his holy name)

way be-yond my wild – est hopes and dreams.

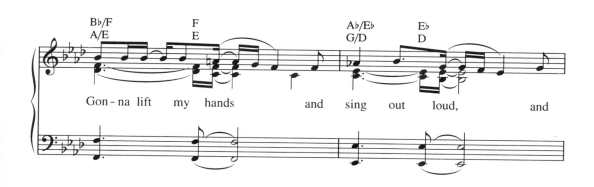

Gon - na lift my hands and sing out loud, and

praise his won - der - ful name. We're gon - na

(Leader)
Hal – le – lu – jah, (All) Hal – le – lu – jah,

(Leader) Glo – ry to Al – migh – ty God. (All) Glo – ry to Al – migh – ty God.

(Leader) Hal – le – lu – jah, (All) Hal – le – lu – jah,

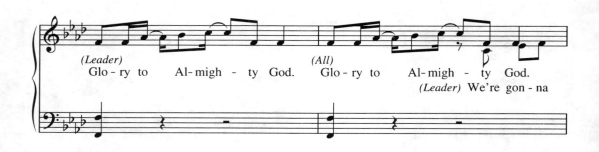

(Leader) Glo – ry to Al – migh – ty God. (All) Glo – ry to Al – migh – ty God.
(Leader) We're gon – na

(All) praise his ho – ly name, we're gon – na

praise his ho - ly name,   lift him up   a-bove the

hea - vens,   praise his ho - ly name.

Words and Music: Darlene Zschech

118 We're not looking back
(Not looking back)

We're not look-ing back, we're not look-ing down,
We're not stay-ing 'round, we're not left be-hind,

we're just look-ing up,
we're just pass-ing through,

step by step and line by line. And it's not by might,

and it's not by pow - er,

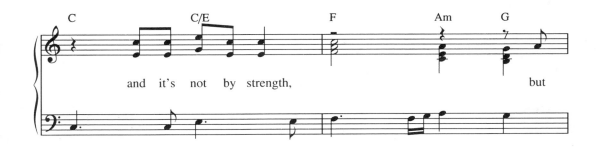

and it's not by strength, but

1.

by my Spi - rit, says the Lord.

2.

by my Spi - rit, says the Lord.

Words and Music: Geoff Bullock

119 We will rise

1. We will rise to take this na - tion,
We aren't fight - ing flesh and blood,

we have come to take this land,
we are put - ting strong - holds down,

we will rise, we have come to take a stand.
we will fight, we will see this bat - tle won.

Lyrics under the music:

We cry lib - er-ty and jus - tice,
we cry right - eous-ness and peace,
we cry free - dom from op-pres - sion,
we pro-claim
thy king-dom come.

2. We have seen the promise and the power,
we have seen his majesty and strength.
In his name, in his name we overcome.
We will see the coming of the kingdom,
we will see the glory of his throne,
we will rise, we will see his kingdom come.

Words and Music: Geoff Bullock

120 We will seek your face
(Touching heaven, changing earth)

We will seek your face, al-migh - ty God,
Fa-ther, let re - vi - al start in us, then

turn and pray for you to heal our land.
ev-'ry heart will know your king - dom come.

Lift-ing up the name of the Lord, in

pow-er and in u - ni - ty. We will see the na-

2. Never looking back we'll run the race,
   giving you our lives
   we'll gain the prize.
   We will take the harvest given us,
   though we sow in tears,
   we'll reap in joy.

Words and Music: Reuben Morgan

I consider everything a loss
compared to the surpassing greatness
of knowing Christ Jesus my Lord,
for whose sake I have lost all things.
I consider them rubbish,
that I may gain Christ and be found in him,
not having a righteousness of my own
that comes from the law,
but that which is through faith in Christ –
the righteousness that comes from God
and is by faith.

Philippians 3:8-9

121 Whatever I have gained
(Lost without your love)

for I am lost with-out your love,

all things are loss

with-out your love.

2. The won-der of your

Words and Music: Geoff Bullock

122 Whenever I see your face

Words and Music: Geoff Bullock

123 With a little love
(Faith)

1. With a lit-tle love, with a lit-tle hope,
2. With a lot-ta heart, with a lot-ta cool,

with a lit-tle light to light the way, faith, the
mind and strength, my trust, my all,

moun-tain will be moved.

With the faith to see me through, ev-'ry moun-tain will

Words and Music: Geoff Bullock

124 You are holy

dee-per in love with you. Here in your courts where I'm close

to your throne, I've found where I be-long.

Words and Music: Reuben Morgan

125 You are my God

Words and Music: Geoff Bullock and Gail Dunshea

126 You are my rock

You are my rock, you are my Lord, a shel-ter from the storm, a light in the dark; and you are my shield, the pow'r of my life, you lit a fire that burns with-in, you are my

Words and Music: Geoff Bullock

127 You are my song

Words and Music: Geoff Bullock

128 You are the one

C
A
Dm
Bm
C/E
A/C♯
F
D
E♭sus4/G
Csus4/E
You are the one, the Word come to life, the
Asus4 A
F♯sus4 F♯
B♭
G
G/B
E/G♯
C
A
Dm
Bm
love of the Fa - ther re-vealed in the Son. You are the one,
Dm/C
Bm/A
B♭
G
B♭/C
G/A
F
D
B♭/F
G/D
F
D
my God, you are the one.

2. You are the one
who calms stormy seas,
who walks on the waters
of my troubles and fears.
You are the one
we find in the fire,
the flame of refining,
the fire of love.

3. You are the one,
the author of life,
creation's Redeemer,
the image of love.
You are the one
freedom proclaimed.
Life everlasting
in Christ has been gained.

Words and Music: Geoff Bullock

129 You give me shelter

Play dotted rhythms as triplets

Words and Music: Geoff Bullock

130 You lift me up

1. You, you lift me up, you touch my soul, you set my feet on high-er ground. And you, you give me peace, the strength of joy like li-ving wa-ters flow-ing down. This is my hi-ding-place, a shel-ter from the storm, a ri-ver of life that floods my soul.

And so I

drink of the wa-ters, I will rest by your streams. Li-ving wa-ters flood my soul, and I can hide in the shel-ter of your faith - ful-ness, liv-ing wa-ters touch my soul. Liv-ing wa-ters touch my soul.

2. You, you pick me up,
   you touch my heart,
   you bring me to a higher place.
   And you, you give me hope,
   this faith in God,
   like living waters flowing down.
   This is my hiding-place,
   a shelter from the storm,
   a river of life that floods my soul.

Words and Music: Geoff Bullock

131 You love me as you found me
(Your love keeps following me)

Words and Music: Russell Fragar

132 You make your face to shine on me
(And that my soul knows very well)

2. Joy and strength each day I find,
   and that my soul knows very well.
   Forgiveness, hope, I know is mine,
   and that my soul knows very well.

Words and Music: Darlene Zschech and Russell Fragar

133 You placed your love

Words and Music: Geoff Bullock

134 You pulled me up when I was down
(You've been good to me)

Words and Music: Russell Fragar

135 You're all I need

Words and Music: Geoff Bullock

136 You rescued me

You brought me life, you made me whole, O Lord, you have

res - cued me. And you loved me be-fore I

knew you, and you knew me for all time. I've been cre -

a - ted in your im - age, O Lord.

And you bought me, and you sought me, your

blood poured out for me; a new cre-a - tion in your im-

- age, O Lord. You res-cued me,

you res-cued me.

Words and Music: Geoff Bullock

137 You're softening my heart
(I surrender)

1. You're soft-en-ing my heart to the know-ledge of your love and o-pen-ing my eyes, you light the way to love you. Words a-lone can-not ex-press all the hope that you have placed with-in me, in be-tween each heart-beat, Lord; I sur-ren - der.

2. Dsus⁴   G/B   *Chorus*   C   Dsus⁴   D

I sur-ren – der   to you,   I sur-ren -

Em⁷   D/F♯   G/F   C/E   G/B

- der   to you   ev-'ry- thing I am and e -ver hope to be;

C   Am⁷   G /D   D

I sur - ren – der   to you,

D/F♯   Em⁷   D   C   G/B   C   G²

to you.

2. You gently pick me up,
wash me with your love,
and opening my ears
you speak the word,
healing, releasing all the hurts and fears
by the hope that you have placed within me,
in between each heartbeat, Lord; I surrender.

Words and Music: Geoff Bullock

138 Your eye is on the sparrow
(I will run to you)

Words and Music: Darlene Zschech

139 Your grace and your mercy

Words and Music: Geoff Bullock

140 Your love is higher than the mountains

riv-ers   lead - ing to the seas.   And

your   love,   no - thing can come clo - ser,
your   love,   there is no-thing strong - er,

no - thing will re - place   it,
no - thing can go deep - er,   who can sep - ar -

ate us from your love?   And

Words and Music: Geoff Bullock

141 Your people sing praises

2. Your people sing praises.
   Let laughter fill the world.
   Your people sing praises.
   Let love and faith be heard.
   Jesus came to the rescue
   and we're the reason he came,
   so come on lift up a mighty voice
   'til Jesus comes again.

Words and Music: Russell Fragar

Index of First Lines, Titles and Recordings

Index of First Lines, Titles and Recordings

This index gives the first line of each song. If a song is known by an alternative title, this is also given, but indented and in italics. A key to the recordings will be found at the end of this index.

Key to Recordings

		CD	Cassette
1	The power of your love (Hillsongs)	HSACD107	HSAC107
2	Stone's been rolled away (Hillsongs)	HSACD101	HSAC101
3	People just like us (Alliance)	ALD076	ALC076
4	Friends in high places (Alliance)	ALD104	ALC104
5	God is in the house (Alliance)	ALD089	ALC089
6	All things are possible (Alliance)	1901302	1901304
7	Shout to the Lord (Integrity)	08952	08954
8	Unfailing love (Kingsway)	KMCD2025	KMC2025
9	Now is the time (Hillsongs)	order direct	order direct
10	The heavens shall declare (Hillsongs)	order direct	order direct
11	Jump to the Jam - Youth Alive (Hillsongs)	HSACD104	HSAC104
12	Worship I (Alliance)	ALD105	ALC105
13	Worship II (Alliance)	1901432	1901434
14	Touching heaven, changing earth (Alliance)	available late 1998	available late 1998
U	Hillsongs Updates (Hillsongs)	order direct	order direct

The recordings listed opposite are available from the following sources:

People just like us
Friends in high places
God is in the house
All things are possible
Worship I
Worship II
Touching heaven, changing earth

Available from your local Christian bookshop, or direct from:
ALLIANCE MUSIC
Waterside House
Woodley Headland
Peartree Bridge
Milton Keynes
Buckinghamshire
MK6 3BY
United Kingdom

Tel: 01908 677074
Fax: 01908 677760

Shout to the Lord

Available from your local Christian bookshop, or direct from:
INTEGRITY MUSIC
Freepost BR1078
Eastbourne
East Sussex
BN21 1BR
United Kingdom

Tel: 01323 431574
Fax: 01323 411981

Unfailing love

Available from your local Christian bookshop, or direct from:
KINGSWAY COMMUNICATIONS
P.O. Box 75
Eastbourne
East Sussex
BN23 6NW
United Kingdom

Tel: 01323 410930
Fax: 01323 411970

The power of your love
Stone's been rolled away
Jump to the Jam - Youth Alive
Hillsongs updates (please state update number when ordering)

Available from:
HILLSONGS AUSTRALIA
P.O. Box 1195
Castle Hill
NSW 2154
Australia.

Tel: 00 612 9634 7633
Fax: 00 612 9634 4591
Email: hillsongs@hillsck.org.au

Now is the time
The heavens shall declare

Available from:
NIGHTLIGHT MUSIC GROUP PTY
P.O. Box 166
The Entrance
NSW 2261
Australia

Tel: 00 612 4334 4155
Fax: 00 612 4334 4151
Email: nightlightmus@compuserve.com

Also available from Kevin Mayhew

The Australian Worship Collection
– arrangements for worship groups.

These complimentary books will be a great addition to the worship group's library. For each song an independent part is given which adds interest for the performer and enhances the beauty of worship.

Currently available in three editions; one for C instruments (flute, violin, recorder or oboe); one for B♭ instruments (clarinet, trumpet or soprano/tenor sax); and another for E♭ instruments (alto/baritone sax, E♭ horn).

Also available from Kevin Mayhew

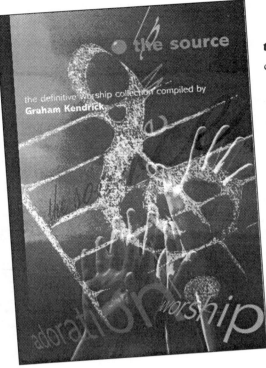

the source
compiled by Graham Kendrick.

Now in its second edition, this definitive worship collection is proving to be a truly international song book, having sold in its thousands all over the world, and received an enthusiastic welcome among church leaders, worship leaders and musicians across a surprisingly broad range of churchmanship and tradition.

Full Music
1470104

Words Only
1470101

The range of worship resources that make up the complete package of **the source** is continually growing, and currently includes:

Arrangements for worship groups – editions for C and B♭ instruments
Acetate masters
CDs and Cassettes

Forthcoming additions to the range include:

Arrangements for worship groups – editions for E♭ instruments
Guitar edition
MIDI files
Song management software on CD-ROM

All of these and our many other publications are available from your local Christian bookshop, or alternatively direct from Kevin Mayhew.

The Easy-to-Play Collections

Easy-to-Play Choruses

A new revised and enlarged edition of the popular collection of choruses scored in easy-to-play arrangements. The number of songs has been increased to 200 to include some of the most popular worship songs of the last two years.

1450100　　　　　　　**ISBN 1 84003 222 7**

Easy-to-Play
Favourite Worship Songs

Updated to include the top 50 songs from CCL's poll of the most popular UK worship songs.

1450102　　　　　　　**ISBN 1 84003 224 3**

Graham Kendrick: His Songs in
Easy-to-Play Arrangements

A collection of almost 100 of the famous writer's most popular songs, including his two most recent compositions *No Scenes of Stately Majesty* and *To You, O Lord*.

1450101　　　　　　　**ISBN 1 84003 223 5**

Graham Kendrick:
His Christmas Songs

19 fine Christmas songs in easy-to-play arrangements, with guitar chords, playable by anyone of Grade 1/2 standard. Includes *Can You See (Song for Christingle)*.

1450111　　　　　　　**ISBN 1 84003 256 1**